Winners Don't Cheat

Advice for young Australians from a young Australian

Sean Jacobs

Connor Court Publishing

ADVICE FOR YOUNG AUSTRALIANS

FOR A YOUNG AUSTRALIAN

WINNERS DON'T CHEAT

SEAN JACOBS

Connor Court Publishing Pty Ltd

PO Box 7257

Redland Bay QLD 4165

sales@connorcourt.com

www.connorcourtpublishing.com.au

Phone 0497 900 685

ISBN: 9781925826029

Front Cover Design: Maya Walker

Back Cover Photo: Jason Tabet

Printed in Australia

About the Author

Sean Jacobs has served as an international youth volunteer, ministerial adviser, Commonwealth public servant, United Nations consultant, security expert, writer and municipal election candidate.

Born in Papua New Guinea (PNG), he has lived in Bahrain, Fiji, Adelaide, Canberra and the Gold Coast.

He holds a BA (International Relations) from Griffith University and a Postgraduate Certificate in Policing, Intelligence and Counter Terrorism from Macquarie University. He also holds qualifications from the Australian National Security College, the Australian Institute of Management and the University of New England.

He has written for a number of publications including The East Asia Forum, The Diplomatic Courier, The International Affairs Review, Policy Magazine, Islands Business, Stella Magazine, Hip Hop Republican and the Australian Institute of International Affairs.

He currently lives in Brisbane with his partner, Eloise, and their pet cockatiel.

Winners Don't Cheat
Short essays in this book

Foreword

Like many of us, I am inundated with emails and the first one I received from Sean Jacobs was certainly in the 'surprise' category. Not only had I never met Sean but there he was asking me to write a foreword to a book I had not even read.

Over a weekend, I read his book of short essays and I couldn't put it down. This is not a traditional book you would expect from someone so young (and sporting dreadlocks!). In *Winners Don't Cheat* he talks about hard work, resilience, not being a victim and how to sensibly approach steady and long run improvement. It has advice from some unlikely places – from not only prime ministers and presidents on different sides of the political spectrum but entertainers, economists, sports stars, business leaders and philosophers.

Sean also talks about his own hard lessons in getting better at writing, the proper way to look at role models, and the difference between education and employability. He has expertly and beautifully written a book of unique messages that every parent should give to their children.

Now it has rarely been 'cool' to be conservative, but Sean realises that the noisy minority need a bit of competition. At a time when many young people are used to hearing about 'rights' *Winners Don't Cheat* puts the emphasis back on 'responsibility'. For young people to become better individuals and members of their community they need to take seriously their own path to self-improvement. Ultimately, this book is full of wisdom that many of us call common sense.

Born in Papua New Guinea, Sean has had quite the life experience – from elite sportsman to a budding public figure with highly positive ideas. He is obviously on his way to greater things. I am sure this book will be his talisman, it will bring him good luck, because he has done the hard work to get him there!

Karl Morris

Company Director, husband and father of five

Introduction

I've always been impressed at how some leaders can articulate your thoughts in a way you couldn't quite express yourself. One person in particular – a United States presidential hopeful from Arizona named Jon Huntsman Jnr – was one of these guys. After watching a video of Hunstman Jnr being interviewed (and speaking perfect Chinese) I searched online for his book. I came up short but found a short self-help memoir by his highly successful father, Jon Huntsman Snr.

Called *Winners Never Cheat*, it's a great reminder of 'old school' values in the cut and thrust of building a multi-billion dollar company. It's a perfect example of how business does not exist as an exercise in greed and exploitation despite what countless young people are told each day. *Winners Never Cheat* tells us not only about the value of business and commerce but underlines that core principles – determination, hard work, skill and integrity – deliver timeless progress, regardless of your complexion or start in life.

Out of some great lessons, however, I found most appealing the title of Huntsman's book, which I've adapted as the headline for this short series of essays. I appreciate the title can be an easy line – a throwaway cliché to dispense but not so simple to follow. But it's a fitting phrase for the themes I've wanted to relay to young people in my decade since finishing school – working hard, orienting toward your passion, appreciating adversity, being a decent person and living with purpose.

As a young mixed-race Australian, I haven't built a billion dollar enterprise, emerged out of poverty or become an Olympic gold medallist. And there are no shortage of marvellous insights from great people who have done all of these things. But world-beating success can seem distant to young people who, so far, have achieved little or are in the immature stages of what they hope is a long and rewarding life.

Although it's taken me some time I've realised that success is like what someone said of prosperity – it's not a line drawn somewhere just above the million-dollar mark but involves choosing your own destiny and living out your potential in your own way. Success is every day, it's personal and it can be threaded into what you're doing right now. You don't need to stand on a podium to experience it.

And it should be recalled that not all of the greats are the most well-rounded people or sustain their hard work over time. Some win gold medals but fail miserably at their marriages, businesses or jobs. Others expose their imperfections through drugs or addictions, while others can just be terrible company around a dinner table.

In my high school years I was a total medium range performer. My average grades culminated in finishing high school with a low-to-middle rank position and being unable to get into university. Friends skated effortlessly ahead into law, science, dentistry, accounting or apprenticeships, all seemingly knowing what they wanted to do and earning good money.

But I took a bit more time to develop. I was a decent water polo player and, after missing out on selection to the Australian Schoolboys team, was personally crushed. I applied for job after job, graduate position after graduate position, and constantly came up short. These seem like trivial problems but, for me at the time, it was heartbreaking at a crucial point in my life.

Fast forwarding a few years, however, I was able to bounce back on my own terms. After completing a bridging course (that my parents supported me through) I barely scraped my way into university, finished an undergraduate and graduate degree, volunteered as an Australian Youth Ambassador for Development to Fiji, consulted for the United Nations in Papua New Guinea (PNG) and then worked as an adviser at the Australian Department of the Prime Minister and Cabinet. I was part of a small team of security planners that delivered Brisbane's G20 Summit and, directly afterward, I was drafted into the Queensland education minister's office as an adviser ahead of the 2015 state election. We surprisingly weren't returned to government but, almost straight away, a security firm tapped me on the shoulder and asked if I'd like to help with their offshore operations in PNG.

I had also journeyed from being a horrendous writer to eventually getting my work published in spaces usually reserved for experts, professors or lecturers. On the sporting front I trained hard in the years out of school and, in 2007, won the Australian national water polo league with my club the KFC Queensland Breakers. It was a surreal feeling.

Sport, of course, is not for everyone. But I found it was a great vehicle for teaching me about adversity. In my final year of high school I remember reading the runner Michael Johnson's *Slaying the Dragon*. At a time when reading a book was a total stretch, turning the pages gave me just enough insight to appreciate that setback and failures were part of the game. I'll always remember Johnson's equation for success: (Natural Talent + Opportunity) x Hard Work = Success. Cheesy, yes, but totally spot on.

At a deeper level I also caught a bug that's essential for progress – an intolerance of my circumstances. Plodding along wasn't for me. I wanted to get out there, work, get better, earn money and ultimately achieve. But I knew the challenges would take time to overcome. It wasn't about beating my chest or punching the air but rather, day after day and step after step, constantly striving to get better.

I don't think that going on to write briefs for the Prime Minister on national security policy, or publishing my experiences on working in international development, was a bad effort for someone who could barely write a sentence without mentally wondering off, whose mind was constantly on the go, and who was too scared to tell people what he was writing about for fear of being judged.

And, as the high school years dipped from memory, I felt I had gone from strength to strength while those sailing past me in school had come to an abrupt halt or had their spotlight turned down. The ones that skated ahead usually got caught up in drugs or seemed to lose any desire or ambition they once held. This is disappointing when considering that, today, there are more opportunities in human history than ever before.

So why did I write these essays? While I'm cautious about using the word 'crisis' in Australia it seems that not just young people but young men, in particular, are in a state of stress. Men, as we know, are more likely than women to drop out of school, suffer depression and commit crime, and they perform more poorly when it comes to academics. While these aren't terribly new insights, technology seems to be the disruptive new ingredient lobbing questions of short-termism, distraction and the search for status at the feet of young men. Many of the experts say that, by increasingly operating digitally, guys are 'wiping out' in the realm of face to face. The Stanford University psychologist Philip Zimbardo concludes that excessive internet usage, video games and pornography have corroded social relationships and driven arousal addictions in young men. 'Addiction you want more', adds Zimbardo, 'arousal you want different.' And today, of course, there's no shortage of choice.

Another destructive factor I see in young people is the combination of shallow materialism and instant gratification. Dangling brightly in front of young people today is what the investment legend John Bogle calls 'the illusory rabbit of success' – wealth, fame and power – and not 'the real rabbit of meaning' – principle, virtue and character. 'It is a poor centre of a man's actions, himself' wrote English philosopher Francis Bacon with great foresight over half a millennium ago.

In terms of responsibility, the statistics, especially around young men, don't entirely paint a good picture. Today in Australia, for example, there are almost a million able-bodied men not working and collecting welfare. I feel that, when we look at statistics like this, not only are ideals of principle, virtue and character on the slide but also concepts of hard work, duty, commitment and sacrifice.

A friend, when reading these essays after I began publishing them in 2015, said that I 'was being strategic'. What did he mean? Like me, he understood that the pull of short-termism and the search for status weren't serving our communities well. It was critical to get out in front of young people, in particular, and provide examples of depth and meaning. The trend of social affairs in this country – expanding handouts, increasing government dependency, over-regulating businesses and slower productivity – mean we need a more resilient and industrious society which, in turn, means more resilient and industrious individuals.

While reading through these short essays many will find that they possess a 'conservative' tinge. What they won't find, however, is an apology for this: I strongly believe that the motivators of success and prosperity – hard work, self-sufficiency and persistence – remain the core turbines of progress despite the comings and goings of new technology, trends or attitudes. If this is a conservative message, then, I welcome the charge.

Done right, correcting the wayward path that young people take is critical. As the American neurosurgeon Ben Carson explains:

> For every one of those young people we can keep from choosing a self-destructive path, that's one less person we have to be afraid of or protect our families from, one less person we will have to pay for in the penal system or the welfare system, and one more productive, taxpaying member of society who may discover a new energy source or the cure for cancer.

Australia, if our best days really lie ahead, needs more discoverers and less destructors. My simple hope is that, from my small collection of essays, I can provide some young people – men or women, boys or girls – with just a grain of insight at what could be the right or useful time. Such a thing, after all, helped me 'stay in the game', get through challenges and move through my early years out of high school with a sense of purpose.

Sean Jacobs, 2018

Blood, toil, tears and sweat

'I have nothing to offer but blood, toil, tears, and sweat,' Winston Churchill famously declared in 1940. He had just been elected Prime Minister of Britain and was speaking of fighting Nazi Germany. But his words remain useful in recognising the sheer grind that is a prerequisite for any success.

Today our sports stars tend to capture the more lively examples of all-out effort. Tiger Woods, for example, spends five hours a day just hitting golf balls on top of an already maniacal training regime. The swimmer Mark Spitz – the Michael Phelps of his day – apparently swam enough laps of the pool to cover the distance of the equator. Daley Thompson, the decathlon legend, famously quipped that he trained on Christmas Days because he 'knew his opponent wasn't.' It should be remembered that training for these folks isn't just a stroll in the park but consists of relentless and carefully calibrated effort.

'Coming early and staying late', as the saying goes, requires an element of persistence beyond simply turning up – the effort must be sustained over time. Andres Ericsson, perhaps the world's foremost expert on performance excellence, says that elite status is built only after years of toil – twenty years, in fact, of what he calls 'devoted effort.' This applies not just to athletes but experts in any field – scientists, doctors, fighter pilots, writers and so forth.

What we often see, and want right now, is the finished product of such toil. Mozart, surprisingly, never conceived his works without great effort. 'Surviving manuscripts,' says Geoff Colvin in *Talent is Overrated*, 'show that Mozart was constantly revising, reworking, crossing out and rewriting whole sections, jotting down fragments and putting them aside for months or years. Though it makes the results no less magnificent, he wrote music the way ordinary humans do.' Mozart, in other words, sweated just like anyone else.

Such examples are found in every arena of endeavour. Former American President Ronald Reagan, for example, was seen as a great 'natural' communicator for his strong messages and smooth public appearances. But, as his speechwriter Peggy Noonan notes, 'he was a natural because he *practiced so hard*.' It's hard to imagine Former President Obama, or any other great public communicator, not doing the same.

Yet we don't have to become President, reach Olympic heights or achieve historical greatness to appreciate that even litres of talent can trickle into mediocrity without hard work. 'Life is a grindstone,' says the television entrepreneur Robert E. Johnson. 'But whether it grinds you up or grinds you down depends on what you're made of.' Much of your effort isn't measured by any public yardstick but by your own internal standards.

This is particularly important to recall when leaving school and entering your twenties. Many of the so-called gifted and talented of our school years have largely failed to reach the Spartan heights they were earmarked for. The main reason they don't, according to Stanford University psychologist Carol Dweck, is 'they may have believed all the hype, the idea that they just have it. And they become afraid of making mistakes. They become afraid of tarnishing their image.' The people who do well out of school, Dweck observes, are 'the people who maybe didn't have an image to uphold, didn't feel the weight of other people's expectations, and just followed their passions and developed their abilities.'

For someone who didn't enjoy strong success when leaving high school I'd add that, in particular, many of my schoolmates didn't quite understand toil. When setbacks arrived I saw that excuses prevailed. Discipline lagged. Drugs took centre stage and the spirit of perseverance faded. Sport, plus a host of other factors, made me appreciate hard work. Certainly, the slogan of 'no pain, no gain' takes on real meaning when your school friends are out partying and you're burning up laps in the pool or the gym.

For many, of course, sport may not be the avenue to appreciate the blood, toil, tears and sweat. We're fortunate to live in a time and place where bombs are not being dropped on our homes – as they were when Churchill gave his golden words. Hard work can be exerted in a library, in a lab, behind a desk, behind a wheel, or in front of a sheet of music or a computer. I have friends, in occupations as diverse as real estate and publishing, enjoying success not only because they appreciate hard work but because they ultimately enjoy what they do. 'If you can find the work you were born to do,' says the rowing champion Steve Redgrave, 'then hard graft never seems like too much of a slog and the fun comes naturally.'

Finding your passion

'Well we sucked,' says the musician Dave Grohl. 'But we loved what we did so we kept playing. But we always found ways to improve… we kept sucking but eventually with improvement we became Nirvana.'

Grohl's simple approach highlights how taking some enjoyment from what you do is vital to propelling yourself to new heights. I use the term 'some enjoyment' because finding your passion is not always an easy or complete endeavour.

Many of my young friends, for example, studied law with ambitions of prowling around the courtroom but ended up 'hating it'. Others started with hands on professions but found that, with experience, they're more cut out for the corner office. Many successful people also say that they 'still don't know what they want to do' even after rising to the top of their professions.

The businessman Russell Simmons thought he found his inspiration through drugs and models – appealing outward signs of success. But, when building his clothing label, he found a sense of 'peace and tranquillity' when marking up sketches and designs. These, he says, 'were the foundations of my happiness and success' and 'not the chaotic life I had created.'

Chasing the appealing outward signs of success, such as a pay rise or fancy job title, will mean little if it's not aligned to your core passion. As the investment legend John Bogle says, 'The point is whether you want to choose the illusory rabbit of success – defined by wealth, fame, and power – rather than the real rabbit of meaning – defined by integrity, virtue, and inner strength.'

So how do you find your passion? Again, it's not an easy or overnight process. But I've found that, especially in your formative years, it's worth exposing yourself to potential opportunities, industries and careers. 'If you don't know better,' says American entrepreneur John Hope Bryant, 'you can't do better.'

Although I didn't know it at the time, a major turning point for me came while visiting Washington D.C. Seeing, as a high school student, the institutions of democracy intersect with foreign embassies, international organisations and professionals doing good work inspired me. Current affairs made more sense to me than rearranging equations in maths class or fiddling with Bunsen burners in the school science lab.

After working across government and non-government sectors in Fiji, Papua New Guinea and Australia 'the dots', to use Steve Jobs' famous words, began 'to make sense.' I won a university academic excellence award, turned around a national sporting organisation in Fiji as part of the Australian aid program, consulted for the United Nations in one of the toughest governing arenas in the world and then wrote policy briefs for multiple prime ministers.

My first years out of school, however, didn't point to such success. Although I didn't get into university on my first go, and there were plenty of rejections to be disheartened by, it was that early experience of 'knowing better' that helped to inspire me. This helped me to take setbacks in my stride, get over my ignorance and, in Grohl's words, 'find ways to improve.'

There was also one critical feature of this growth – I worked hard to build skills. This, as the American professor and self-help guru Cal Newport emphasises, is more important than taking leaps at what you think is your passion, especially when you're young and starting out. It's much more advisable, says Newport, to 'focus on getting good' and then using the career capital this generates to build a career.

I've heard many young people complain about their perceived lack of capabilities. But, as the actor Stephen Fry points out, these people usually have no problems reciting 'hundreds of pop lyrics and reel[ing] off any amount of information about footballers, cars and celebrities.' Being interested, he says, enables such young people to suddenly call upon their supposedly absent capabilities.

I've also heard many young people complain about a perceived lack of opportunities. But there is, literally, no better time in history for young people to find or chase their passion. We live in an era, to paraphrase the comedian Chris Rock, where the best golfer is a black guy, the tallest basketballer a Chinese guy and the best rapper a white guy. The pathways open to us are what previous generations could only dream of.

General Colin Powell, when asked if he knew that he would go from sweeping floors to serving as US Secretary of State, said that he didn't know such prospects existed in his early years. What he did, however, was build on the things he enjoyed while working hard, constantly preparing and learning from failure. The success, over time, found itself.

If you can't immediately find your inner calling, or don't know exactly where you want to go, Powell's lesson offers very simple but decent advice. With a journey of steady improvement, and an exposure to and realisation of opportunities, you may not exactly find your passion, but you'll equip yourself with a solid foundation for long term success.

Leaders are readers

'Not all readers are leaders,' said American President Harry Truman, 'but all leaders are readers.'

Truman, who never went to college, is a great example of a self-taught and historically consequential leader. Able to read Thucydides and Cicero in the original Latin, Truman was apparently so up-to-speed that he once even corrected a Chief Justice of the United States.

Painted as a buffoon by the so-called intellectuals of his day, Truman's supposedly poor decisions – to fight the Korean War and pursue a strategy of containment against the Soviet Union – have since been vindicated by history. Because Truman could look further back, some say, he could see further forward. But he could only 'look further back' because he was a great reader.

The point of Truman's story is to show not just the value of reading but how central reading is to leadership, especially at the highest and most critical levels. The former American President George W. Bush famously competed in reading battles against his top adviser, Karl Rove, where the President read well over 50 books a year – from writers like Albert Camus and Abraham Lincoln to topics like the Soviet Union and the Spanish Civil War.

Bush, I believe, is the Truman of our time – a leader who, through his own efforts at reading and self-education, made the tough but ultimately right decisions of his day.

Away from the realm of American Presidents you find other leaders making the same effort at constant self-education and reading. Mexican telecommunications billionaire Carlos Slim is apparently surrounded by stacks of books and constantly reading. Carlyle Group founder David Rubenstein apparently 'reads dozens of books each week.'

You also hear of busy leaders finding time to read at any chance they get – Rupert Murdoch, for example, devouring Nick Cater's *The Lucky Culture* in a single plane trip. Or Australia's former chief public servant Peter Shergold doing the same with James Button's *Speechless*.

The benefits of reading are obvious – it helps to build verbal range, assimilate new information, reduce stress and even increase emotional intelligence.

Another benefit is that anyone can do it. I read around eighty books a year mainly because it's the easiest and most immediate way to develop my knowledge. As the former slave and great American educator Booker T. Washington asked: 'Do you love learning enough to walk ten miles to borrow a book you cannot afford to buy? And having no money for books, will you borrow the texts and memorise your lessons?'. Serious readers answer yes to these questions. These days, with our unprecedented access to books, there's little excuse not to read.

But apparently we're doing it less. And the chief consequence, I feel, is ultimately greater ignorance. The historian Niall Ferguson, for example, when speaking to groups of financial leaders, usually asks how many of them have read *The Monetary History of the United States* and *Golden Fetters*. Only one in a hundred hands appear, he says, despite these books being classic texts on financial crises and economic depressions. You would expect more from financial experts. 'The only history they know,' Ferguson suggests, 'is the history of their own careers.'

Decision makers, of course, must know the consequences of their actions, especially at critical times like responding to financial downturns and other economic turbulence. Historically, there is no shortage of poor decisions that have been aided by ignorance. Imagine, for example, the carnage that could've been spared if Hitler's early territorial expansion had not been appeased by war-weary allies. Imagine, too, if Truman had not made his tough but resolute decisions to fight against North Korean expansion. There's a good chance that, today, there would be no South Korea. 'Those who cannot remember the past,' as the saying goes, 'are condemned to repeat it.'

Reading gives me a perspective on history, provides insight into human nature and helps to dissolve ignorance. It also shows that most bright new ideas have, especially in the world of government, been tried before. This is particularly important in the political arena where young people constantly fall for 'hope and change' without appreciating the grain of human nature, ideas like self-interest and the unique Western inheritance of personal liberty, scientific expertise, political democracy, and free markets.

This is not to say that reform is pointless, or to fall for the foolish notion that everything has been invented. Rather, it is to recall the timeless value of reading summed up by the late American humourist Leo Rosten: 'Men die; devices change; success and fame run their course. But within the walls of the smallest library lie the treasures, the wisdom, and the wonder of man's greatest adventures on earth.'

So how do you read more? Obviously find books you enjoy. But I'd say that it's important to take the time to read things other than the fiction of JRR Tolkien, Stephen King or JK Rowling. 'Biographies of great, but especially of good men,' said Scottish author Samuel Smiles in the late 1800s, 'are nevertheless most instructive and useful, as helps, guides, and incentives to others.'

Good advice. But I only got it by reading.

Circumstances and race are no excuse

What's interesting from reading about success is the sheer number of people who have risen from nothing. The universal stories of people lifting themselves from humble circumstances, in all sectors, at different times and of all different skin colours, is so common that it's almost banal.

Yet young people, particularly minorities, are continually sold a picture of despair. A few years ago I attended Indigenous Australian cultural awareness training that presented a circular diagram called 'the poverty wheel'. This unbreakable and frustrating loop, garnished by references to historical and cultural considerations, laid out the setbacks that young black Australians face. 'Why bother?' it seemed to ask – the cycle simply couldn't be broken.

I wondered what Booker T Washington or Frederick Douglass – Americans who had risen from slavery to statesmen – would think of the poverty wheel. Or George Washington Carver, the great American inventor, also born a slave. I wondered what America's first female black astronaut, Mae Jemison, would think of it. Or Colin Powell, going from sweeping floors in a bottling factory to a four star general and US Secretary of State.

Ironically, just after the cultural 'training' session, I went straight to the library and accidentally came across the biography of Australia's Neville Bonner. Here was an Indigenous Australian – born under a tree in the early 1900s, enduring countless rounds of real discrimination and hardship – who reviled self-pity and resentment to become Australia's first black federal parliamentarian.

'A most prevalent cause of failure,' says Dennis Kimbro, is 'the use of race, sex, or circumstances as a reason for inactivity.' I've seen countless people, not just young minorities, disqualify themselves because of these reasons. When unloading shipping containers for spare money I was always amazed at how the guys around me viewed this work as their destiny. For me, studying and always reading about a world of possibilities, the work was only temporary. But, for many of them, going beyond these circumstances wasn't worth it.

In some youth minority circles, in particular, it's common to hear that finishing high school or pursuing certain professions is 'not for us' – a view based entirely upon complexion and circumstances rather than any real examination of individual capability or passion. Young minorities often spend a great deal of time contemplating what 'the group' will think if they follow something that interests them, or if they dare to study, follow a passion other than sport or read books.

Compounding these problems are young people who, basing their desires only on people who look like them, worship instant gratification over any sense of grit and persistence. From clothing to attitude, everything for these young people runs counter to building professional or social skills useful in the real, modern world. Achievement is scorned rather than promoted. Ideals of real character, like John Paul Jones' timeless and universal traits of a naval officer – tact, patience, justice, firmness, kindness, and charity – are harpooned and even mocked as unsuitable for their lives.

On a deeper level, some intellectuals and social commentators do their best to reduce Australian history to just a series of racially-based events and tag our institutional inheritance as the legacy of 'old white men.' Added to this ash heap of despair is the notion that the free market is simply a casino where luck is awarded over merit, skills and excellence. For crime and anti-social behaviour some fumble around for every kind of excuse where blame is prescribed to a range of 'factors' except the person that actually threw the punch or stole the car.

How is any of this useful in getting beyond difficult circumstances? Belief, I feel, is what it comes down to. Albert Einstein said that the first and most basic question all people must answer is 'Is the world a friendly place?'. If young people decide that the world is unfriendly then, most likely, that's what the world will be – offensive, unequal and unfair. But there are three things to remind young people who think that they can't claw themselves out of despair or tough conditions.

First, orienting toward success is made easier by following some basic benchmarks. An instructive study from the Working Seminar on the Family and American Welfare Policy says that if you finish school, try to stay employed, get married and avoid criminal behaviour, you're bound to avoid long-run poverty. Such benchmarks, it seems, are not terribly rigorous.

Second, the groups that have generally done well tend to follow certain attitudes and priorities. Successful minorities, for example, from Chinese Americans to Indo-Fijians, have generally reviled self-pity, disliked blame, doggedly pursued education, spent wisely and constantly sought ways to provide a service or deliver goods that people want. Constant favours from government, 'leg ups' or specially designed welfare programs have played a very limited role in their advancement. But self-help has.

Third, character requires no money. 'Can a poor person be a gentleman?' asks a young schoolboy in Lloyd Jones' *Mr Pip*. 'A poor person most certainly can,' replies the boy's teacher Mr. Watts. 'Money and social standing don't come into it. We are talking about qualities. And those qualities are easily identified. A gentleman will always do the right thing.'

'To want to be ambitious and to want to be successful is not enough,' reflects the actor Kevin Spacey. 'That's just desire. To know what you want, to understand why you're doing it, to dedicate every breath in your body to achieve... If you feel you have something to give, if you feel that your particular talent is worth developing, is worth caring for, then there's nothing you can't achieve.'

Absent from his advice are circumstances or race. This is what our young people need to hear, not tired excuses like the poverty wheel.

Building wealth and financial freedom in your twenties

Written with input from Jordan Shopov

For young people today the idea of building wealth can be daunting. Never in history have we been so well off but, at the same time, so overwhelmed by financial advice. A dizzying suite of credit cards, savings funds and mortgage offers mix with technical terms like 'derivatives' and 'negative gearing' to present a confusing picture of the world of finance.

Ideas like saving and 'thinking long-term' in your twenties can be difficult. And, without putting your money to use, a decade can pass with little to show other than a pile of debt. But the path to wealth and financial freedom is made much simpler by considering just three basic steps.

Step one is to avoid debt. The investment legend Warren Buffett says that the biggest suggestion he has for young people is to 'avoid credit cards.' It's simply impossible, he says, to get ahead by paying 16-18 percent interest. To avoid debt some people cut their cards up, others use debit cards (so they actually have the cash first) or just enlist self-control in exchange for impulsive buying and poor decisions.

Step two is to spend less than you earn and invest your savings. Spending less than you earn doesn't always mean tightening your belt but sorting out what's central to your life and what isn't. An education, for example, is probably an area where you want to spend money versus a holiday in the Bahamas. And when you take time to examine what you spend money on, versus what you actually need, it's amazing how much income can be spared.

In terms of investing your savings it's not optimal to just place cash in a savings account – your money needs to go up in value not just when you work but even when you sleep, eat and relax. Pouring money into a savings account can also be outpaced by inflation.

One of the ways to beat this, over the long run, is by investing in an index fund. As Buffet's business partner Charlie Munger says: 'If you consistently spend less than you earn and invest it in index funds... in 20, 30, or 40 years, you can't help but be rich.' The secret to this is called 'compounding', which Albert Einstein said was 'the eighth wonder of the world.' Compounding basically allows you to earn interest on interest. When you add time – something young people have an advantage in – to a good rate of return we have the 'magic of compounding.'

But today, more so than ever, young people are animated by the idea of instant gratification – wanting something now rather than having to put in the years of hard work. The pervasive use of credit creates a warped picture of wealth where consumption can be done now but kicked down the road and paid for later.

Television shows tell young women that, by writing a weekly column, they'll breeze through life in a multi-million dollar New York mansion wearing the latest, most stylish and expensive clothes. Young men, meanwhile, are led by a similar instruction that building a tech start-up can be done out of a garage almost overnight, or that dropping out of school is a sure-fire way to success.

Movies, too, sell a popular overnight version of financial success that seems to revolve around speculation (*Wolf of Wall Street, Wall Street: Money Never Sleeps*), or outright gambling (*Runner Runner, The Gambler, 21*). It's easy to be seduced by the financial alchemy of complex algorithms, chart patterns, insider trading, or counting cards. Ultimately, however, it is character that builds real wealth and value in society.

This relates to the third and most important step, and one which many older people say they wish they had in their twenties, which is to operate according to your 'inner-scorecard.' In other words, to maintain a consistency between your work, life and core values. This may seem more like a piece of self-help rather than financial advice but the two are inherently inter-connected. Poor life choices and irrational decision-making are the fastest track to unhappiness and financial ruin.

Buffett and Munger's great success, both in life and in business, stems from a complete lack of contradiction between their personal values and life choices. This is why they have often attributed their wealth to a 'temperamental advantage that more than compensates for a lack of IQ points.' The goal, therefore, is not to strive for success as measured by others, but to do the work that best suits you. Wealth will inevitably be a by-product of such personal fulfillment.

For those who doubt this mantra, Buffett poses the following question. 'Would you rather be considered the best lover in the world and know privately that you are the worst, or would you prefer to know privately that you're the best lover in the world, but be considered the worst?'

Staying power

In my late teens my Mum gave me a book titled *The World at Their Feet* edited by Australian writer Claire Halliday. It has some great insights from young actors, doctors, specialists and writers that have built and enjoyed success early in their careers. One contribution is from the fashion designer Kit Willow, then just twenty-eight, on creating her own fashion label. Here she is worth quoting at length:

> I worked on it for a year – just me in my spare bedroom. It was really very lonely because I was working on a concept and an idea all on my own and there was no one there to support me. Every day I'd wake up and walk into the office and I'd be the one who was instigating every little thing that was going to happen that day. That can be really confronting and really exhausting. It doesn't give you a chance to sit back and rest, or to reflect on what you've been doing, or even the way you've been doing it. The phone's not going to ring without you making it. You just have to keep plugging away every day.

Through hard work and passion Willow created a global brand – great success for someone in her late twenties and in such a competitive industry. But, in 2012, after spending time at international prominence, she was dumped from her own label.

Willow's story is typical of the temporary nature of success. She may not have lost any of her passion or desire for hard work but, as any young professional will learn, what gets you to the top may not necessarily keep you there. Circumstances change and new challenges arise but it's important that you stay ahead or on top of them.

This is observable not just with people but also in business. The first printing press, produced by German Johannes Gutenberg in 1455, was historically pivotal in starting the printing industry but was immediately edged out by competition. By 1469, twelve printing companies had been established and the industry had moved from Germany to Venice. What happened to the companies? 'Nine of them were gone in just three years,' writes the economist Tim Harford, 'as the industry fumbled for a profitable business model.'

Like today, things were highly competitive. 'The higher the atmosphere,' writes the late academic Herbert Aptheker, 'the more difficult it becomes breathing.' Although 'eighty per cent of success is showing up', you obviously must do more than 'show up' to do well. Young people will quickly learn that landing a dream job, winning a championship or scoring well on a test simply opens up more doors and challenges.

Since leaving school I've found that there are five broad points that are worth considering on how to stay at the top of your game.

First, keep on learning. This may mean a new course, upgrading a certificate, self-education through reading or emerging through any experience that truly expands your horizons. When working in the Pacific Islands, for example, I enrolled myself in a Postgraduate Certificate in Policing, Intelligence and Counter Terrorism. Many thought it was strange but, a few years later when working for the Australian National Security Adviser, the qualification was more than useful. A trait of successful people is a commitment to life-long learning.

Second, re-invent yourself but stay true to your core skills. 'The best way of attaining enduring success,' writes five-time Olympic rowing gold medallist Steve Redgrave, 'is to find a role for yourself where your skills fit the opportunity.'

An instructive example of this from the business world was Intel founder and CEO Andy Grove who, under intense pressure, moved his company from manufacturing memory chips to producing microprocessors in the 1980s. In his book *Only the Paranoid Survive* Grove described the process of re-invention as a 'strategic inflection point' where the rules of the game suddenly change and leaders have to make critical and often wrenching decisions. Rather than lead Intel into an area in which its expertise was not transferable – they suddenly didn't start making aeroplanes for example – Grove successfully changed Intel's direction while staying in the high-end technology sector.

Suddenly wanting to be an engineer, even though you're terrible at maths or hate numbers, probably requires some reflection. As is wanting to be an NBA star but only being five and a half feet tall.

Third, staying power requires positive reinforcement. As you get better your confidence may improve but even the best still get jitters and need constant reinforcement. It's great to build skills but they don't always stick. You must reflect on success but use it to build new mental strengths and as a continuous source of inspiration. Furthermore, you can't rely on the approval of other people to do what you are passionate about or think is right.

Four, don't let standards slip. A telling insight from Australian cricketing legend Steve Waugh reveals how even letting small things slip is enough to cause a dip in elite level performance. 'It all boils down to attitude,' reflects Waugh on a particular rough patch facing the team. 'In our case, attention to the little details had ceased to be a priority. Punctuality had slipped; the intensity of our training had diminished; the banter and encouragement in and around the group had waned. Not by a lot, just enough. We needed to get back to basics and do the things that had made us successful in the first place.'

Five, continue to work hard. The late publishing legend John Johnson said that he celebrated his success in the old fashioned way – he worked. The political scientist Charles Murray says, in laying out his tips for the next generation of young and ambitious, 'Here's the secret to remember whenever you hear someone lamenting how tough it is to get ahead: Hardly anyone works as hard as he or she could. The few who do have it made.'

The interesting case of role models

For young people, role models can be powerful and inspirational figures. They help us to look down the road and see what it takes to reach the high plateaus of success.

Around three years out of high school, when just starting my undergraduate degree, I finally stumbled on the realisation that, to get ahead, I had to actually get better. This may seem obvious but it meant more than I anticipated – I had to improve my writing, listening and presentation skills. This, in turn, meant I had to get better at attention to detail, concentrate harder and become better organised.

This was helped considerably by 'thinking with the end in mind' and looking closely at the achievements of successful people. What characteristics did they exhibit? What did they do to get ahead?

But I didn't set my sights on the Richard Bransons or the Bill Gates of the world – I examined relatively quiet achievers like White House Fellows, the candidates of the most competitive graduate programs and people close to me that had done well. All toiled away without the glare of the public spotlight. Their lessons were clear: apply yourself, achieve fine benchmarks and build skills. Doors open just that little bit further, it seems, when you do these things.

Such minor details are important when looking at role models, who can be great at showing us the big picture but not always useful when we're trying to imitate their attributes or achievements in our day-to-day lives. It's tough, for example, to hit golf balls for five hours a day like Tiger Woods. It's tough, as South African golfer Gary Player says, to then bandage your hand from the bleeding and go out and keep hitting. It's tough to stay up reading, highlighting passages and note-taking when you're tired and needing sleep. It's tough to jump into cold water each morning to train for years upon years without awards or fanfare.

In applying the lessons of role models, you shouldn't be distracted from your own goals, capabilities and attitudes. If you doggedly follow someone you look up to, it's easy to get carried away with their success and not your own carefully calibrated standards. Aptitude and slowly finding out what you're good at are key in this process.

When studying international politics at university, for example, I certainly wasn't going to win an academic scholarship. And I wasn't even sure I liked writing. But additional effort, with some generous marking from tutors, gave me a taste of what it'd be like to score half-decent grades, which felt good and kept me motivated to take further steps toward achievement.

We should also remember that some role models carry plenty of unvarnished traits that don't always meet the public eye. And nor does their current success mean future success. The most admired role model in 1971 among American school kids, for example, was OJ Simpson. At one stage, around one-fifth of National Football League players were competing with criminal records, while out of wedlock births – disastrous for a good start in life – are supposedly rife among the many stars of the National Basketball Association. One sports agent, for example, claimed he spent more time dealing with paternity claims than negotiating contracts.

At the end of the day, as important as role models are, it's individuals who must commit to the process of improvement. Simply pointing to a hero and saying, 'Look, do what he's doing,' is simply not enough. Asserting your own initiative is critical.

On a wider level, and across all different contexts, we see this 'disconnect' taking place all the time. Many thought, for example, that a black American president would reduce black crime when the reverse has actually been true. The economist Walter Williams takes this further. Installing black leaders, he says, to key positions like police chiefs and town mayors, has not remedied any of the well-being indicators of blacks in these places.

Certainly, it can be comforting to see someone like you that has done well. 'Everybody needs to see a version of themselves do something,' says the comedian Chris Rock, 'it's just good, it makes you feel like you can do it.'

But the lesson for all young people is – don't find role models that only look like you. There are literally tens of thousands to choose from. Personally, for example, I'm motivated by the logic of neuroscientists like Sam Harris, the perseverance of political leaders like John Howard, the written words of soldiers like Patrick Leigh Fermour, and the courage of political pioneers like Neville Bonner. Never does a role model have to look like you, or be from your sector, to help inspire your own path to achievement and success.

Resilience: why you need it and how to get it

In 1984 British Prime Minister Margaret Thatcher was in the fight of her political life. In 1979 she had inherited a Britain divided not only by crime and terrorism but also facing the twin challenges of astronomically high inflation and unemployment. This meant that, each day, people's money was becoming increasingly worthless and there were no jobs for millions of Britons.

Pinnacle to her challenges, however, was a coal industry that was unproductive, costing huge amounts of taxpayer money and acting as a drag on the British economy. Each time Thatcher proposed putting more people into work, or shutting down an unproductive mine, she encountered furious union opposition and 'outrageous displays of union muscle.' In 1984 she wanted to shut twenty (and eventually seventy) mines but came across the same expectations of union friction – picket lines, disruptions to businesses, mass strikes and police clashes.

A stalemate ensued but eventually the unions, used to having their way and bringing down previous governments, voted to return to work. Thatcher, as many say, eventually won 'the war of attrition' and turned around the British economy through her free-market reforms, tax cuts, privatisations and reigning in of government spending. She is a pivotal figure in world history not just for these economic reforms but also for her immense contribution to global security in helping to defeat the Soviet Union, hardly a small feat, and crushing Argentina's military aggression in the Falkland Islands.

Her performance during the 1984 miners' strike is an instructive lesson in overcoming adversity but not in the way you might think. Thatcher clearly needed huge amounts of personal resilience to deliver the reforms she believed in. However, central to her strategy during the early years of her tenure was to build up coal reserves in advance of waging the battle she anticipated she would have to have with the unions. This meant that when the fight she had prepared for did arrive, the unions could strike for as long as they wished but they could not hold Britain hostage.

Life, I cannot help think, is like that. When hitting bumpy patches we need to call upon our own reserves to weather the storms. But many young people today, it seems, don't 'do' bumpy patches well. Terrified of hurting young people's feelings, we're accustomed to a climate where 'everyone gets a medal' and participation is usually rewarded over performance.

To build resilience it's fundamentally important to get comfortable with failure. Literally every person that has enjoyed success knows, and continues to know, failure in some way. The earlier we can learn this lesson the better.

Giving up or walking away, when you think about it, is actually the most logical response to defeat. 'It's human nature to quit when it hurts,' writes Seth Godin in *The Dip*. 'But it's that reflex that creates scarcity.' Since leaving school I've learned that rewards come if you stay in the game and double down, work harder, smarter and continue to improve.

When I was in high school I had the publically trivial but personally crushing experience of not being selected for the Australian Schoolboys Water Polo Team. I had trained much harder than anyone in my team, was one of the fittest players at the tournament, top-scored, and played out of my skin. I was shocked and humiliated when my name wasn't called out for selection.

Thankfully the support of strong parents and a sports mentor dragged me through the short-run pain. And I ended up learning some important lessons that have helped me later in life – take nothing for granted, work hard and make every post a winner because, even when you've thrown everything at a challenge, there are things that are simply out of your hands.

And from this comes another great lesson – you can't control other people's decisions but you can control how you react to them. This certainly doesn't take the sting out of defeats. But feeling like you've made a choice enables you to approach bad news with a sense of confidence as you push forward to your next setback or challenge.

In the years that followed I trained harder, got smarter and improved. It wasn't until four years later that I won a national water polo championship. It was a surreal feeling – better, I think, than making the Australian Schoolboys Team would have been. Again, rewards come to those who stay in the game and double down, work harder, smarter and continue to improve. I've replicated this approach to everything I've achieved so far.

Many young people will face their own unique challenges. They are, in the end, your own and many will not understand the fuss. But how you respond, says the former slave and American Presidential adviser Booker T Washington, 'is the ultimate determining factor between success and failure.'

Another way to build resilience, on top of learning from failure, is through relentless 'preparation' and 'hard work'. The saying that 'most battles are won when people aren't watching' perfectly sums up the role of preparation and its link to resilience. By preparing day after day you're ready for the tough challenges that lie ahead. And by working hard you're used to plugging away, even when no one's watching or patting you on the back.

The future will reward young people who have boundless resilience. 'You learn ten times more in a crisis,' says Procter and Gamble CEO AG Lafley, 'than during normal times.' So, like Thatcher building coal deposits to save Britain, young people must build resilience by drawing upon their resources, learning from failures, preparing and working hard.

Becoming decent at writing

In 2006 a university lecturer told us that if there was anything to 'get' out of a university degree it was to become a decent writer. Doing so, he added, would make our professional lives much easier.

Almost a decade into my career I've seen his point validated more times than I can recall. From writing policy briefs for Australian Prime Ministers to slide presentations for Fijian swimming coaches, I've seen that reaching a decent standard of writing is a key skill in many professional (and even personal) arenas.

Getting there, however, is tough. At least I found it so. Submitting assignments and other written pieces over the years I always believed I had delivered world-shifting prose matched with unique insight. My tutors, I thought, simply didn't know what good writing was. Like the fool driving down the wrong side of the road, and thinking everyone else is crazy, this process was an example of ignorance at its finest.

Taking feedback about your writing is hard because, quite simply, it means putting your ego in the back pocket. And it means a sobering reflection on current capacities. But it's here when you can start to get better. 'Once I realized how little I knew about writing,' says the prolific writer and economist Thomas Sowell, 'I could start to learn.'

Despite being a hard path to follow I've strangely found that, perhaps more than any other skill, writing is incredibly easy to work on – you don't need a swimming pool, a running park or a gym. From sitting on a bus to lying in bed, writing can be worked on at any time. Here are a couple of simple things that have helped me so far.

First, I've found examples of decent writing and cherished them. We all have passages, writers and turns of phrase that tug a chord with us. I say 'cherish them' because, without recording them, you will inevitably forget. I tab up each book or article I read with mini post-it notes (or the highlighter on kindle), then take notes and save them on my computer.

I obviously extract more from some books compared to others in terms of literary value and writing content. I took about 2,500 words of notes from Nick Cater's *The Lucky Culture*, for example, but only 600 words from Rupert McGuiness' biography of the rugby player George Smith. This process is certainly not fun but it helps me improve.

Second, I continue spending a huge amount of time reading and building knowledge. It took me about four years of reading around fifty to seventy books a year before I thought seriously about submitting something for publication. And even when I did I was knocked back.

Third, find your authentic voice. I enjoy travel writers like the late Patrick Leigh Fermour but, in the end, I could never write like him. His swashbuckling and enchanting words are great to read but simply aren't for me to put on paper. I enjoy the beauty of plain writing.

Expanding on this idea of 'your authentic voice' the late Christopher Hitchens, a formidable speaker and writer, gave the following advice to his writing classes:

> I told them to read every composition aloud, preferably to
> a trusted friend. The rules are much the same: Avoid stock

expressions (like the plague, as William Safire used to say) and repetitions. Don't say that as a boy your grandmother used to read to you, unless at that stage of her life she really was a boy, in which case you have probably thrown away a better intro. If something is worth hearing or listening to, it's very probably worth reading. So, this above all: Find your own voice.

Four, I've learned to write for the right context. Policy briefs, for example, are not places where you drop the names of scholars and extend sentences to meet word counts. Universities and schools, however, are places where you might have such latitude. Like my first point above, cherishing or mimicking good writing is achievable in any arena. Get hold of good memos, letters, briefs, emails, invoices or business plans and try to mimic their coherence and layout.

The most obvious mistake I've been guilty of, and continue to see, is wordiness. We've all read lengthy emails and wondered why they're so long but say so little. 'Apologies. I have made this letter longer than usual because I lack the time to make it short,' wrote French mathematician Blaise Pascal over three centuries ago. Learning to use fewer words takes time but it can be a great way to improve your communication skills, get exactly what information you need to complete tasks and increase your own productivity.

The last activity that's helped me to improve my writing is simply giving myself time to keep revising and crafting. A few years ago a submission I wrote to the Australian Institute of International Affairs Emerging Scholars Series was knocked back. I felt totally dejected but, for the better part of the next year, I worked hard on another paper. Day after day, week after week, I continued to shape and recraft.

The editor changed just one word of my new submission. This is a good testament not just to bouncing back from rejection – an experience all great writers endure – but simply giving yourself time to sharpen up your written words.

Finally, better writing can lead to a better mind. It was said of Malcolm X that, with books and reading, 'the honour roll student reappeared and the layers of street life faded.' My writing story has followed a similar theme. Improved writing has helped me to lay out thoughts, be more methodical and refined the delivery of my message.

Aptitude

A few years ago a blunt and stunning passage by the late Australian philosopher David Stove caught my eye:

> If you are recruiting potential basketball champions, you would be mad not to be more interested in American Negroes than in Vietnamese... Any rational person, recruiting an army, will be more interested in Germans than in Italians. If what you want in people is aptitude for forming stable family-ties, you will prefer Italians or Chinese to American Negroes. Pronounced mathematical ability is more likely to occur in an Indian or a Hungarian than in an Australian Aboriginal. If you are recruiting workers, and you value docility above every other trait in a worker, you should prefer Chinese to white Americans. And so on.

Stove's words are typical of a thinker truly committed to discussing 'the things we think but do not say.' Critical, witty and obviously direct, not everything he wrote earned him prominence or broadened his legacy. 'Stove,' as American art critic Roger Kimball reflects, 'would not have been made to feel welcome at many American colleges or universities.'

But his point didn't ruffle me or cause offence – as it all too easily would have for so many these days. It got me thinking about the idea of 'aptitude'. Clearly, just by way of being human, we're all born with an orientation toward some things over others. 'Of course,' writes the psychologist Carol Dweck, 'each person has a unique genetic endowment. People may start with different temperaments and different aptitudes, but it is clear that experience, training, and personal effort take them the rest of the way.'

As young people we need to sharpen up and focus on what we're good at, especially if we want to avoid mediocrity and the easy path of just plodding along. 'The problem with coping,' writes Seth Godin in *The Dip*, 'is that it never leads to exceptional performance.' Not thinking seriously about your skills, and what you want to do, is a gangplank to average performance and not getting the most out of life.

Exploring your aptitude is, ultimately, a lot like finding your passion – some serious discovery is required. What do you love to do? What would you do for free? What comes easily to you but harder to others? How do others view your talents and gifts? Such questions, even if you can't answer them in full, will help tease out your aptitudes. The less you kid yourself in this process the better.

Having a career that swings between high-level policy and being 'on the ground', what I often find among successful people is that they tend to enjoy the day-to-day versus the title of the job. This means they may draw satisfaction from things like working in a team, providing direction or having autonomy.

Others, however, enjoy working individually or deferring decisions to others. Writing invoices, for example, may not exactly enliven small business owners. But, hidden beneath the surface, processes like relationship building, generating a service and delivering on commitments give them a sense of satisfaction.

Another consideration to make, once you have an idea of what path you want to pursue, is calibrating the odds of success in your chosen field. Modern life, with all the trimmings of instant gratification, offers fame, fortune and power as the objectives of success. Young people often gravitate toward glamourous professions – actors, musicians, entertainers and so forth. There's nothing wrong with this as long as they understand the likelihood of success. The 'safer bet' is much more useful to think about, as Dennis Kimbro reveals in his advice to young black Americans. Here's what he means:

> In 1992 there were 337,178 black schoolteachers, 68,590 black engineers, 25,704 black lawyers, and 18,795 black physicians plying their trades – many rather successfully – throughout the nation. Now contrast these numbers to the actual figures that blacks constitute in pro sports: National Football League, 789; National Basketball Association, 243; major-league baseball, 163.

You don't have to aspire to glamourous professions to enjoy professional satisfaction or even great wealth. Whatever path chosen – carpenter, doctor, pilot or sports star – the common theme tying all of it together is to not simply rely on talent. This is what Carol Dweck means in her comment above when she says that 'experience, training, and personal effort take them the rest of the way.'

Talent can never be relied on to go far. In fact, the consensus among all the greats is that hard work beats talent. This is why many of those who excel at school, whether in the classroom or on the sporting field, tend to burn out once they emerge into the competitive world.

The last point I want to make here is that, even when you've found your craft, don't neglect other areas of your life. Obsession can be a great thing, as the legendary rugby coach Clive Woodward explains, by helping 'in the long hours of practice.'

But something that took me time to realise is that we're not all heroes at everything. In high school, for example, when reading about Michael Johnson, I was amazed that he could run 400 metres faster than anyone in history but, when he applied his Herculean work ethic to studying maths, he'd barely pass his classes.

This, I thought, was an anomaly. Surely world-beaters are good at everything they do? Then, sometime later, I began hearing of other examples. Michael Phelps, for instance, is the most successful Olympian ever but showed impeccably bad judgement by smoking marijuana and drink driving. In other arenas the personal choices of people like General David Petraeus and Tiger Woods didn't so much detract from their public achievements but added to my thoughts that even world-beaters aren't maestros at everything.

If you're not a top performer now but have some idea of what you're good at, or can be good at, recognise that it's your personal business to make it happen. If you find your aptitude, and then work hard on it, you're guaranteed to do well.

Hygiene, self-regard and public appearance

I've always thought it's strange that 'hygiene' rates a mention in many older self-help books.

'I sometimes feel that almost the most valuable lesson I got at the Hampton Institute,' reflected the former slave and American educator Booker T Washington, 'was in the use and value of the bath.' Thus basic hygiene, clean teeth, a good haircut, and general presentation, became core themes of Washington's education to ex-slaves at his famous Tuskegee Institute.

'Hygiene' itself certainly seems like an odd topic today. But public health, of course, is nothing like it was in the late 1800s. Polio, Tuberculosis and other diseases cut through entire populations in the then-developed world.

While diseases have abated, however, the appearance aspect of 'hygiene' remains incredibly important. 'In order to get a job in today's tight economy,' says one writer in the Tuskegee Observer, 'a healthy smile and a professional appearance can mean the difference between being hired and being passed over for another candidate.'

One thing any young person will notice is that the majority of successful people dress well or spend a great deal of time on how they look. It was recently revealed, for example, that the late British Prime Minister Margaret Thatcher underwent a staggering 118 hair appointments in just twelve months. Underneath her no-nonsense public demeanour existed a deliberate and exquisite care of appearance. 'See her,' to paraphrase Ralph Waldo Emerson, 'and you will know as easily why she succeeds, as, if you see Napoleon, you would comprehend his fortune.' As a young man I've often heard that it doesn't matter what you look like – it's what's on the inside that counts. I thought like this for a while, especially in my first years out of school, yet I slowly sensed it wasn't quite right. Eventually I stumbled upon the British writer Theodore Dalrymple's similar observation. 'If profound and clever men did not care for their appearance,' he wrote, 'then not caring for one's appearance meant that one was profound and clever. It took me quite a time to appreciate the fallaciousness of this so-called reasoning.'

Being well dressed, therefore, evokes self-regard. 'Looking good,' says the former Olympic sprinter Linford Christie, 'means feeling good.'

It's interesting to note that, regardless of how much money you have, a good public appearance is not beyond reach. It tugged on my heart strings reading that Neville Bonner, Australia's first black federal parliamentarian, had his mother cut up a flour bag and make it into a shirt on his first day of school. Feelings of self-decency, and not circumstance, drove this desire.

In those days – 1930s Australia – even the simplest public tasks had to be performed with impeccable appearance. My own late grandfather, for example, used to always wear a suit into town – a widely practiced social routine he carried with him his whole life. 'I have been deeply moved to see the old men of deeply-depressed towns,' adds Dalrymple of his days in Southern Britain, 'who themselves lived very hard lives, and who were the most working of the working class, dress smartly in ties, jackets and highly-polished shoes merely to go to the pub for a pint of beer or to do a bit of shopping.'

Having spent a great deal of time in the South Pacific I've also seen very poor people in these places, regardless of their circumstances, taking an equal measure in their appearance. 'Having lived among really poor people in Africa and elsewhere,' adds Dalrymple, 'I know that to present a good appearance to others is for them a triumph of the human spirit and not just a manifestation of vanity or superficiality.' Such efforts are a strong testament to doing the best you can do, even without having much.

So if young people are to present well, then, what are they supposed to wear? Without delving too much into fashion advice I can't help but notice that the greats tend to emphasise a sense of modesty over being too 'loud' or tacky. 'Avoid bright colours,' counsels Booker T Washington. One of the most pivotal figures in world history, Martin Luther King Jnr, apparently owned six suits – four black and two grey. 'Conservative at best,' writes Dennis Kimbro. Indeed, I feel there's something commanding about being smart but not too eye-catching or pretentious.

I would also suggest dressing 'up' rather than 'down' for most occasions. It's easy to tone it down, of course, if you've overdone it. And as Condoleezza Rice, the former US Secretary of State, recalls in advice from her mother, 'Condoleezza, if you are overdressed, it is a comment on them. If you are underdressed, it is a comment on you.'

My advice to young people is to present themselves well but also agonise over building character. This is because character, ultimately, is reflected in your presentation. 'Do not be content to wear silks and diamonds on the body,' said American author Orison Swett Marden, 'to tide around in your limousine, and to dress the mind in calico and character in rags. Let self-improvement, self-culture, a healthy mind, a fine personality be your richest dress.'

Staying out of prison? Odd but good advice

Clayton Christensen, the Harvard innovation expert, delivered an insightful speech a few years ago titled 'How will you measure your life?'

Christensen, with unique perspective and a strong business mind, prompts his Harvard Business School (HBS) students with three questions: First, how can I be sure that I'll be happy in my career? Second, how can I be sure that my relationships with my spouse and my family become an enduring source of happiness? Third, how can I be sure I'll stay out of jail?

This last question, he says, is far from flippant. 'Two of the 32 people in my Rhodes scholar class,' he notes, 'spent time in jail. Jeff Skilling of Enron fame was a classmate of mine at HBS. These were good guys – but something in their lives sent them off in the wrong direction.'

It's not hard to see people of iron will and heroic achievement – the Lance Armstrong's, David Petraeus' or Tiger Woods' of the world – possessing obvious flaws in their character. In their own lives, too, young Australians will notice people who possess fine attributes and amass impressive achievements but run into similar bother.

The path to prison is less obvious than committing a crime. It simply starts with bad choices, which is something everyone is capable of regardless of their station in life. I can recall multiple times, for example, where young professionals have come to me asking if they should do something that they know isn't the right thing to do in the workplace. This usually involves a superior asking them to lie to a customer or someone else in the organisation. At these times I always think of Christensen's advice and the fate of brilliant people, like Enron's Jeff Skilling, who slide down the slope of poor choices.

Cutting corners in the short-term spells long-run misfortune. Christensen, for example, talks about 'marginal costs' – an economic term for looking at the cost of alternative decisions. 'The marginal cost of doing something wrong "just this once" always seems alluringly low. It suckers you in, and you don't ever look at where that path ultimately is headed and at the full costs that the choice entails.'

So how do we avoid bad choices? It starts with a combination of vigilance and principles. Christensen, who has been religious for most of his life, gives the example of his religious commitment to not playing basketball on Sundays. When he first said 'no' his teammates and coach were understandably both angry and confused. But had he said yes, or simply agreed to play just a few times, it would've set a precedent. 'Had I crossed the line that one time,' he says, 'I would have done it over and over in the years that followed.'

A couple of other examples I enjoy are from the professional life of black American economist Thomas Sowell. Sowell, who didn't exactly have a successful start in life, emerged as a prominent American economist in the 1970s. Twice he turned down great professional opportunities, at consequential times in his career, because they were based on skin colour over merit.

The first is when a young Sowell, just after completing military service, is overlooked for a job as a photographer in America's all-powerful National Security Agency (NSA). Sowell, after discovering that the job strangely became 'closed' after the NSA learned he was black, notifies his Congressman of the clear racism. Surprisingly, not long after, he's asked to come in for a full tour of the NSA and is offered the job on the spot (a job that, mysteriously, has re-emerged). When Sowell attempts to give the interviewer samples of his work he's told that he doesn't need to. 'The job is yours,' says the interviewer. 'No, thank you,' Sowell replied. 'I don't want it that way.'

The second example is where Sowell, much later in his career, is offered a place on the editorial review board of the American Economic Review, the most prestigious economic journal in the world, by Nobel Prize winning economist Kenneth Arrow. But Sowell declines when discovering that the offer is not based on ability but efforts to 'racially diversify the membership of the board.'

Avoiding bad choices doesn't always require a laser-like focus on principles but can also be found in simply doing the basic things right. There's one statistic from the United States that speaks volumes about making simple life choices to stay out of trouble. According to an astonishing study by the Brookings Institution you are almost certain to avoid poverty in a place like America if you: finish school, get a full-time job and wait until age twenty-one before getting married and having children. This, I can't help but feel, is the same lesson in Australia.

'You've got to define for yourself what you stand for,' says Christensen, 'and draw the line in a safe place.' Early in your career do your absolute best to say no to unethical behaviour and bad decisions, regardless of how minor. I'm certain that you'll thank yourself in the long-run. This will not only help refine your principles and assist you in making good choices but, as strange as it may sound, stay out of prison.

Principles first, methods second

What I've found over the years, from a career bouncing across sectors and countries, is the importance of core principles. What do I mean by principles? I simply mean a set of beliefs, values and, in a good old-fashioned way, actually standing up for something.

I feel that young people today have the idea that principles are only for the rigid self-righteous types or aren't useful for an innovating, modern world. But, looking at things more closely, principles are actually essential in two areas – navigating complexity and responding to change.

After a few years of working across a number of policy areas I discovered the importance of teasing out my own set of instinctive beliefs. In government, in particular, I found myself bombarded with complexity. Facts, figures, tables, opinions and other information was placed at my feet, which was all designed to help me arrive at the best decision on what path to take. I found that, on any complex issue, it's easy to be overwhelmed.

But principles can help. It was said of former Prime Minister John Howard, for example, that he broadly approached new policy ideas with the following three principles in mind: does it strengthen the family, expand the scope for private enterprise and encourage individual choice?

Clearly this approach didn't turn out too badly – Howard's reign led to record economic growth and employment, no government debt (a surplus in fact), productivity growth, tax reform, ground breaking gun control, the liberation of East Timor and a virtual end to illegal maritime arrivals.

Not all issues, of course, can be examined this way. And those on the opposing side of politics might suggest that 'social justice' and 'fairness' are better yardsticks for assessing new policy ideas. But, largely because of his principles, you knew where Howard was likely to stand on matters of public interest.

Principles are important not just in running a country but also in our everyday lives. Hard work, persistence and personal responsibility are all principles which, as any successful person can attest, can carry you a long way.

But embodying all of these values will not shield you from failure or the myriad of challenges life throws one's way. This raises another area where principles are important – understanding and responding to change.

Some principles, at least those I subscribe to, recognise that some parts of human nature are very difficult to change. Thomas Sowell's maxim that 'there are no solutions, there are only trade-offs' tends to capture how I think the world works. 'Whatever you do to deal with one of man's flaws,' Sowell adds, 'it creates another problem. But that you try to get the best trade-off that you can get. And that's all you can hope for.'

Without wandering too much off topic, any look at human history validates Sowell's conservative beliefs and values. The point here, especially when it comes to our everyday lives, is that we need a healthy appreciation of what's likely to work and what isn't in trying to get better, work on ourselves and pursue our goals.

Therefore, it's important to know when to change tactics but, at the same time, always stay true to your principles. Steve Jobs, in building Apple, was forced to constantly make trade-offs but stay true to what he was trying to achieve. 'I'm actually as proud of many of the things we haven't done,' he said, 'as the things we have done.'

Should you compromise your principles? 'Never,' said the late US Supreme Court Justice Antonin Scalia to a group of high school students. 'Unless, of course, your principles are Adolf Hitler's. In which case, you would be well advised to compromise your principles, as much as you can.' His point, although flippant, suggests that it's more about the quality of your principles versus the voracity of your beliefs.

'The man who grasps principles,' wrote Ralph Waldo Emerson, 'can successfully select his own methods. The man who tries methods, ignoring principles, is sure to have trouble.' Young Australians can read up on any of their heroes. They'll find that, deep down, they're all guided by a strong set of beliefs. This not only helps them navigate complexity and respond to change but also weather the inevitable storms that come from generating progress. The sooner this can be grasped in life the better.

The need for mobile individuals

'He is as comfortable in a church pulpit,' observed Bill Clinton's adviser Stanley Greenberg, 'as in a Wall Street conference room.'

Politics aside, Greenberg's description of the former American President is instructive for the kind of individuals we'll increasingly need in Australia. Australia's social and economic trajectory demands young people who can acquire portable skills, generate strong networks and produce outcomes across sectors.

One of the most lethal developments for a society, and indeed for a nation, over the long run is for people to stop reaching out, interacting and speaking to each other. Our leaders often talk about 'social cohesion' in the same breath as economic growth because, quite simply, it's as important. For a nation to work its individuals must ultimately share values.

However, despite advances in social media and greater opportunities to 'connect', it is actually easier than ever to live atomised lives where people stay in their closed groups. 'Organisational membership is down,' records the Australian politician and economist Andrew Leigh. 'We are less likely to attend church. Political parties and unions are bleeding members. Sporting participation and cultural attendance is down. We have fewer friends and are less connected with our neighbours.'

It's important to remember that one's degree of social connection or mobility is rarely based on wealth. It is found more, I believe, in the lifestyle one chooses to have – for example, the importance one accords to religion, one's social tastes, the activities one pursues and so forth.

I feel that truly being mobile means being able to connect with people, which at its core requires real compassion and affinity. These virtues, I sense, are what enable 'mobile' people like Bill Clinton to feel comfortable among others regardless of the setting. 'All my life I've wanted to be involved with people and help them with their problems,' says Clinton. 'I've been interested in all kinds of people. Politics has just given me a way to pursue my interest and my concern on a large scale. I've given it all the energy and spirit I can muster; I've tried to bring out the best in people through politics; and I've really been very happy doing it.'

What has helped me build compassion and affinity? Besides genes, which have a lot to do with the values you form, I was fortunate to also have a cosmopolitan upbringing. I was born in Papua New Guinea to my Papua New Guinean mum and Australian dad before spending ten years growing up in the small Middle Eastern kingdom of Bahrain. Sitting cross-legged in class I can still recall my Indian, Pakistani, American, British, Egyptian and Libyan schoolmates, many of them also mixed-race, building that same process of affinity. Dad was a pilot and, when not visiting Australia, I was even luckier to travel throughout the region, Africa and parts of Asia. These exchanges didn't always mean a cultural tolerance of everything I saw in some parts of the world. But they have given me some sense of familiarity and acceptance when moving in different circles.

Compassion and affinity can, of course, be easily cultivated without an expanded cultural horizon. When I came to Australia for high school I made a conscious effort to try different activities. I was a lousy academic student but I took part in everything from sports to learning guitar to drama to training in the army and air force cadets.

When emerging from school and hitting university I noticed that young people tended to cocoon themselves, pursue their own interests and increase their isolation. Again, like my school days, I worked hard at showing up to different events and trying different things even when I wasn't naturally enthused about them. I helped organise public speaking competitions, worked as a sports development officer around Queensland's schools, doorknocked on campaigns, performed fundraising for my water polo club and engaged in other activities that weren't entirely fun but meant 'getting out there' and seriously 'giving things a go'. This required no smarts or savvy. And it was very useful in generating professional and personal networks, which came in handy later.

Besides compassion and affinity, building mobility also means seriously being able to exchange ideas. Unfortunately, from my experiences with many young Australians, the capacity to consider different points of view is in serious deficit. It's rare, for example, to hear balanced opinions from students on sensitive public issues like climate change, refugee policy, terrorism and capitalism. The only remedy I can suggest is for young Australians to read more books and speak to more people, both of which, thanks to technology, are easier to do than ever before.

Ultimately, being comfortable with different ideas isn't just nice to have – it's an economic necessity. 'The free exchange of goods and ideas,' writes the Australian journalist Nick Cater, 'are the natural distributors of wealth and knowledge.' As a result of unprecedented affluence our interests are more diversified and increasingly specific. This has created demand for all kinds of individually designed products and services that competitive young Australians will need to meet. It means a future of smaller companies, more entrepreneurs and, in American media mogul

Mortimer Zuckerman's words, a demand for 'the upstart, the rebel, the young, and the innovator.'

Welsh historian Jan Morris, describing the World War Two soldier and writer Patrick Leigh Fermour, provides a gentle but spectacular example of a mobile young man that applies across generations and despite the trappings of new technology:

> He is Everyman, but in a particularly delightful kind. People of all sorts like him. He makes friends wherever he goes, is as polite to tramps as he is to barons, repays all his debts, shows just the right degree of diffidence to his seniors, merriment to his peers, flirts with girls who give him duck eggs, gets drunk, hates hurting people's feelings, and altogether behaves as a clever and gentlemanly young Englishman of the 1930s ought to behave.

There are immense opportunities for competitive young Australians who can exhibit not just affinity and compassion but use these virtues to be mobile, move across groups and seek opportunities in a changing economy. And possessing such characteristics will help to assure Australia's social cohesion and economic growth well into the future.

Give him a boatload of money

'If you ever want to see someone be great at what they do,' says the NBA superstar Kevin Garnett, 'give them a boatload of money or anything they wish for and see if they go at it the same way as if they didn't have anything.'

In school I can recall the painful and sweaty experience of hiking up hills on school camps. With maps and compasses in hand we'd clamber to the top of a hill and, thinking we were at the summit, almost collapse at the sight of another hill before us. This, our smiling instructor advised us, was a 'false crest'.

It's the perfect term, when leaving school, for staring at the path ahead of you and calculating success. If only, I remember thinking, I could *just* reach a certain income or get a job then all my problems would be solved. My friends and I believed that whatever sign of success it was – a car, winning a competition, a high paying job, a qualification or a girlfriend – if we could just get to a certain stage then it'd all be okay. We would've 'arrived', we thought, and our problems would've abated.

Except, as many young people will find out, this isn't how things work. False crests are everywhere in your younger years. 'One-off events do govern much of our happiness at a given moment,' says American academic Arthur Brooks, 'but the impact of each particular event is surprisingly short-lived.'

I only appreciated this after a few years of professional life, emerging from a few challenges and tracking down my goals. Don't get me wrong – achieving goals was exhilarating and satisfying. But big wins, as Brooks suggests, don't translate into long-run momentum. 'Lottery winners report a big happiness boost at first,' he says, 'but actually end up less able to wring happiness from simple pleasures and ordinary events than nonwinners.'

'Don't bet your happiness on big events,' adds Brooks. 'If you count on the big brass ring to make you happy, you'll only find frustration.'

So what makes us happy? This is a question that, despite its lofty and elusive nature, has actually received a tremendous amount of research. According to studies the four basic things that bring the most happiness to most people are faith, family, community and work.

However, it's important to remember that you have to work hard at all of these things. There's a trap in thinking that, if you just let these things boil away, you'll simply feel good about them. Having a good career, for example, clearly requires effort if you're going to get ahead.

And, clearly, no one can enjoy opportunities by an endless existence of working for free or without the eventual help of money. 'They say money can't buy happiness,' says the writer PJ O'Rourke. 'But it can rent it.' O'Rourke's point, although flippant, is important. An emphasis on making money and creating wealth shouldn't be shied away from but encouraged because money, ultimately, makes life easier and enables opportunities.

Yet using money as a prime motivator is a recipe for misery. Your toil and hard graft must give you enjoyment, fulfilment and satisfaction. If making money was what success meant, I was fortunate to learn from my Dad, then superstars like Tiger Woods would've retired a long time ago. A life of painful training and nerve-splitting performances simply wouldn't be worth it.

Although it's taken me some time I've realised that success is like what someone said of prosperity – it's not a line drawn somewhere just above the million-dollar mark but involves choosing your own destiny and living out your potential in your own way. Young Australians shouldn't be fooled by false crests. Chase down your goals but don't rest on them. Realise there's more work to be done and, whether it's in faith, family, community or work, success and happiness require constant effort.

Is the small stuff important?

Young people will often hear conflicting advice about whether the 'small stuff' is important. As a schoolboy, for example, I was encouraged to think about the 'big picture'. But I also recall being told I should focus on the 'day to day' and 'not get too carried away' with the larger elements beyond my immediate control. This applied to everything from personal finance tips like saving through to advice on how to advance professionally.

Without approaching these two bits of advice with some experience, however, they can be intensely confusing. What is the 'small stuff'? We usually take it to mean the tiny inconsequential matters chewing up our time at the expense of focusing on big deliverables. The financial advice guru Ramit Sethi provides a great example about sweating the small things when trying to save money:

> It's easy to talk about cutting back on lattes, disabling the oven light to save $0.03 over 2 years, and never ordering appetizers. Great! You'll save $11,000 in 30 years and hate yourself every day of your life... None of us wants to live like a penny pincher. Do you really want to know how to make your own laundry detergent and save $0.32/year? Who wants to live like that?

It's much easier, he says, investing early, focusing on getting a dream job, starting a side business or optimising your credit. In other words moving away from the 'small stuff' and focusing on 'big wins'.

Young Australians will hear a similar philosophy in the professional arena. 'Don't get beaten down by the minutiae of day-to-day life'. 'Get used to imperfection'. And, as the title of the late Richard Carlson's bestseller suggests, 'Don't Sweat the Small Stuff'.

Indeed, there's a great deal of benefit in thinking this way. But I've found that the day to day also matters a great deal. I can recall a few times, in fact, when 'not sweating the small stuff' put me in a bit of bother and led to lousy outcomes.

First, I thought such advice meant being careless about minor details. When writing assignments or other professional documents (cover letters, briefs etc) I thought that a mistake here or a mistake there wasn't worth much – the big picture took precedence over the seemingly minor. That was until poor grades and red marks came back all over my work.

In another example, when working for the United Nations (UN), I remember not doing a small piece of work in the lead up to a regional policy workshop. It's not that the task didn't come up – I thought about it regularly. But I carelessly left it alone. My supervisor, as you can imagine, wasn't impressed on finding out that the task was incomplete.

Clearly, as these examples show, I was incorrectly interpreting the small stuff. These tasks, although seemingly minor, were actually incredibly important to achieving bigger objectives. I've discovered that appreciating the small tasks you're asked to complete comes from understanding where both big and small things matter. By thinking with the end in mind, for example, or understanding where my efforts properly fitted into the wider picture, I could now see where the small pieces of the puzzle became critical.

The professional term for this is 'strategic thinking' and, as one manager explained to me, it's what it takes to start emerging upward in the workplace. Knowing where your efforts fit in requires the right balance of vision and plain old experience. If I were to go through school and university again I would sweat small details like my assignments and other written work. And, when confronted by even a small amount of responsibility, like organising that UN workshop, I would go at it harder and not let anyone down. 'If you can't be trusted with small matters,' asks US Supreme Court Justice Clarence Thomas, 'how can you be trusted with important ones?'

You don't have to wait for such learning experiences to come to you. If you want to know what's down the road, as the saying goes, ask the person who's coming back. Enlist your supervisors, mentors and others around you to help canvas the bigger picture. You can even learn a great deal from people who do the wrong thing. This will help to clarify where you can add value and enrich your contribution. It'll also make even mundane tasks tolerable and help you move up the ladder. Both the big and the small stuff matter.

Education versus employability

As a former policy adviser to a senior state education minister I've been to many graduation ceremonies. These are obviously proud moments not just for students but for parents and friends. A qualification, as multiple university lecturers reminded me, is tremendously important in a competitive, globalising world.

Yet I've often thought about the education that doesn't come in a classroom or that isn't easily transposed onto paper. This is an education with a great deal to do with you as a person rather than your formal pedigree. Being book smart, for example, doesn't always translate into street smarts. And education doesn't always mean employability.

We now have a situation in Australia where many young people are going to university for the sake of simply getting a degree rather than looking at the job market and seeing where their skills or aptitude match up. 'Half a million graduates (more than 20% of the total),' according to the Australian researcher Peter Saunders, 'are currently unemployed or doing jobs for which university qualifications are not required.'

In the United States many observers are now sounding alarms on what they fear is an emerging education bubble. Skyrocketing costs of formal study, paired with unreal expectations of a college degree, are not only fanning student debt (US1.2 trillion) but producing a surplus of graduates without the appropriate skills to generally do well in the professional world. 'College,' says one observer, 'is becoming the new high school.'

My sense is that we'll eventually see something similar in Australia. But an education bubble will simply pronounce two trends already in demand – hands on qualifications and online institutes (like the Khan Academy or Alison). Demands for skilled workers, like electricians and nurses, will not abate despite the overemphasis on a Silicon Valley inspired future of gizmos, holograms and robots. In fact, economic trends, such as an orientation toward smaller companies, will necessitate more entrepreneurial, risk-taking, ambitious and mobile young Australians: working among people, in other words, versus hiding behind desks, certificates or qualifications.

Simply training for training's sake is not likely to go far in any professional arena. Real skills, at the end of the day, lead to real jobs.

What's truly required for life, says the Indian writer and statesman Shashi Tharoor, is a 'well-formed mind' and not a 'well-filled mind'. What does he mean? A well-formed mind, says Tharoor, is a mind that 'reacts to unfamiliar facts and details. That can synthesize information that it hasn't studied before. A mind, in other words, that can react to the bigger examination called life that doesn't only give you things you prepared for.'

Failure is how well-formed minds are sharpened. 'I have studied in many schools,' said the American activist Malcolm X. 'But the school in which I studied the longest and learned most was the school of adversity.' While Malcolm X is remembered for his radicalism and a divisive philosophy he is less well-known, in the words of American academic Jeffrey Harris, as a decent example of 'positive initiative and self-discipline for independent study.'

What I enjoy reading about most are highly successful people

who have risen entirely through self-education. Everyone, of course, is self-educated in some way. But the examples I enjoy, among countless others, are the stories of people like Paul Keating, Thomas Paine and Harry Truman. Keating, a former prime minister and treasurer, never finished school but led the transformation of the Australian economy. Paine was a corset-maker but wrote *The Rights of Man* – one of the most influential books of all time. And Truman never went to college despite being one of the most consequential American Presidents in history. There are endless examples like this not just in our history books but in the successful people around us.

Rarely some figures come along who can combine lethal book smarts with street smarts. Here we find people like Winston Churchill, for example, who married an impeccably sharp brain with hard-won experience. 'By the time he was twenty five,' according to Boris Johnson in *The Churchill Factor*, 'he had become a Member of Parliament, written innumerable articles, delivered many handsomely paid lectures, and reported from multiple war zones.' But it wasn't just a life of academia, books and comfort. Churchill knew the rougher edges of not just failure but combat by possessing 'the unique distinction, as a prime minister, of having been shot at on four continents.'

What practicality or a sense of 'street smarts' gives you, on top of confronting adversity, is a capacity to work with people while adding value – a key combination of skills for young Australians to gain. 'Be the person your colleagues and bosses trust to get the job done,' says the career consultant Vickie L. Milazzo. 'When you become someone people rely on,' she adds, 'they won't hesitate to move you up in the company or to recommend you to people in their networks.'

Young Australians should never be so ignorant to turn down a chance for a good formal education. To get my foot in the door, after all, a degree was essential. And the stats (for now) say that getting a degree, on average, means a better income. But I soon realised that, to actually be employable and useful in the professional world, formal credentials need to come equipped with skills that aren't taught in a classroom. Combining book smarts with street smarts will not only mean a 'well-filled mind' but also help young Australians ignite a decent and rewarding career.

What reforming the NYPD can teach you about self-improvement

A story I've always been fascinated by is New York City's crime turnaround. In the early 1990s the city had over 2000 murders a year. By 1997, however, the number of murders had dropped to less than 800. Other crimes, from public vagrancy to assaults, descended to record lows over the same period. New York, from its globally notorious reputation as a violent and dangerous place, emerged to become the 'safest city in America.'

Central to this success were the reforms undertaken by Republican Mayor Rudolph Giuliani and his first New York Police Department (NYPD) commissioner William J Bratton. Bratton, dubbed 'Robocop' for his no-nonsense policing tactics, advocated cleaning up the city's public places, putting more officers onto the streets, swiftly prosecuting offenders, enhancing community expectations and actually enforcing the law over extending even greater leniency to offenders.

'No police department in the country has come close to achieving what the NYPD has,' reflects the policy analyst Heather MacDonald. 'Today, 10,000 minority males are alive who would have been killed by now had New York's homicide rate remained at its early-1990s levels.' This is clearly an astonishing achievement.

But there are lessons here not just for crime-fighting. To complete their turnaround the police had to apply discipline, be realistic about what they could and couldn't do, undertake constant self-assessment and pay attention to the small things. Applying the same strategies in your personal or professional life will also take you far.

In terms of applying discipline, the NYPD had to get serious about dealing with the public effects of poor private choices. The late seventies, Bratton writes, 'was an anything goes era. Marijuana and hallucinogen use was widespread. Under the banner of freedom of expression, society was becoming increasingly tolerant of aberrant behaviour becoming so commonplace that society excused it.'

Citizens, and not just the police, simply became fed up. Countering this meant putting cops back onto the streets, not turning a blind eye to crime and actually enforcing the law rather than persisting with the attitude of 'anything goes.'

Even in our personal lives a similar intolerance can be a great motivator in saying 'enough is enough' and putting us on a path to discipline and resolve. Victor Macfarlane, for example, the highly successful American real estate developer, built his entire empire from an intolerance of his boyhood poverty. From humble beginnings he made a conscience decision that being poor would no longer pay a price in his life.

In my life I can recall simply being fed up not with poverty but mediocrity. While at university, for example, I was sick of writing poor assignments. So, while reading as much as I could, I studied good essays and mimicked their coherence and structure. It took time but, like any skill, I eventually got better. Grades went up. Satisfaction improved. And, along the way, I turned out to be an okay writer.

Any degree of self-discipline, according to the great self-help guru Orison Swett Marden, includes a step toward self-mastery.

'Such self-training, such self-conquest,' he wrote in one of his many classics *Iron Will*, 'gives one great power over others. It is equal to genius itself.' Discipline will not only help you get things done but also get noticed. The US Supreme Court Justice Clarence Thomas, for example, says that the major difference between the young law professionals that clerk on the Supreme Court and those that don't boils down to self-discipline. 'By self-discipline,' he adds, 'I mean doing what you are supposed to do and not doing what you aren't supposed to do.'

The NYPD in the 1990s also became fiercely realistic about what they could achieve. Bratton, as a career policeman, knew there were things he simply couldn't change about his colleagues. 'No one in professional policing,' he wrote, 'has been able to change the police officer's developmental pattern from idealist to realist to cynic.'

Like any good strategy Bratton started with taking stock of where things were before setting a path to improvement. 'I came up with a 46-page course of action,' he reflects. 'We identified the department's major strengths and weaknesses, defined its role within its parent agency, identified the changes needed to bring the organization into the modern world, and, most important, developed a written statement of its values.'

In developing our goals or refining our aspirations we also need to be serious about what's achievable. Importantly, Bratton didn't simply foist the strategy upon colleagues or the organisation. He carefully examined what was 'considered by officers most important to the NYPD' and 'what officers considered was most important to themselves.' Officers, he found, most wanted to 'reduce crime, disorder and fear' but felt that the organisation wanted them to 'stay out of trouble', 'hold down overtime' and 'write summonses'.

Only once these organisational and personal gaps were closed could the results become achievable.

A similar balance of capability and aspiration is required for setting personal goals. But crafting your own strategy must align with your inner passion otherwise, simply, it won't work over the long-term. This really comes down to asking yourself some simple and sobering questions. What do I want to do? What would I do for free? What am I good at? What am I lousy at?

Self-knowledge, of course, requires self-assessment. Another question to ask on your path to improvement is – how do you know that you're getting better? The NYPD, while unfolding their new crime fighting strategy, constantly analysed their own performance. Crime statistics, under their famous 'COMPSTAT' process, were broken down by precinct. At regular meetings crime data was brought up on a big screen and, when the time came, relevant officers were held rigorously accountable for the statistics in their area.

Experts call this process 'deliberate practice'. Whether flying an F22 Raptor or learning to draw for the first time, this involves countless hours of careful repetition and, of course, expert coaching. Although we can't use deliberate practice for absolutely every process in our lives, following a COMPSTAT-like mechanism of accountability and feedback can help. The periods where I've most improved, for example, have been when, at the end of each day, I've purposely reflected and looked at the things I did well and where I could improve.

Finally, the police had to sweat the small stuff. 'During the early stages of the initiative,' says Bratton, 'we found that one out of every seven people arrested for fare evasion [on the metro] was wanted for some warrant for a previous crime. One out of twenty-one was carrying some type of weapon, whether a box cutter, a knife, or a gun… now were beginning to understand the linkage between disorder and more serious crimes… every arrest was like opening a box of Cracker Jack.'

Paying attention to the detail, in any arena, is important. Once you have a good idea of where you're headed the small tasks, although seemingly inconsequential, can emerge as incredibly important. Doing 'the small stuff' right can not only assist your long-run strategy but help stoke self-discipline and tease out other timeless values like delayed gratification, self-reliance, prudence and foresight.

Today, there are less than 400 murders in New York City each year. This suggests that the police have not only been able to keep crime down but achieve what I feel is another essential to real success – sustain results over the long-run. People will be able to do the same if, just like the NYPD's seismic turnaround, they apply discipline, are realistic, undertake self-assessment and pay attention to the small things.

Goals: the ember in the ash heap

In around 2004, at the height of violence and carnage in Iraq, the town of Fallujah was described as 'the ember in the ash pit of the insurgency.' I remember thinking that, despite its context, it served as the perfect metaphor for your goals and aspirations. Because despite the noise, the doubts and the circumstances that inevitably batter your path to success, what's truly important to you will sustain itself.

Since leaving school ten years ago I've noticed that highly successful people often talk about a 'destiny' or an 'inner calling' propelling them through the inevitable peaks and troughs. Success to these people isn't a matter of 'if' but 'when'.

Take, for example, the acclaimed actor and performer Jamie Foxx. 'When I was growing up in Terrell, Texas... there was something inside telling me I would go far,' he says. 'It's like energy – an intangible destiny.' Richard Parsons, the former Chief Executive Officer of AOL Time Warner, puts it another way. 'I always knew I'd rise to the top,' says Parsons, 'it never occurred to me I wouldn't.'

Such statements, of course, appear arrogant. Yet there's more at play here than destructive self-confidence. These people, I feel, have simply connected large reserves of self-belief with inner passion. They march toward what's important to them – their goals – with not just a sense of fulfilment but destiny.

How do they find what's important to them? It starts, says American author Robert Greene in *Mastery*, with an early inclination. The basic elements of all the great masters in history, he observes, consist of 'a youthful passion or predilection, a chance encounter that allows them to discover how to apply it, an apprenticeship in which they come alive with energy and focus.'

While I certainly don't consider myself a 'master' in any sense, finding my own passion for history and politics followed a similar early inclination. For as long as I can remember I've been interested in current affairs. As a youngster growing up in Papua New Guinea (PNG), the Middle East, and in South Australia and Queensland, current affairs was an area in which I showed a degree of strength compared to science, maths and economics. Knowing where countries were on a map, or the dates of historic events, slowly graduated into a deeper understanding of the workings of government and free enterprise. Naturally I aspired to a career in the public sector because, simply, that's where my inclinations lay.

Once you have found this orientation your goals can begin to take shape. The idea of setting goals is incredibly simple – create a target and lay out the steps to get there. But I've found, in the decade since leaving school, it's not something that can be achieved in a five-minute workshop (as we were often encouraged in school). Goals need to be calibrated over time and they must mean something to the only person that matters in the process – you.

After finishing university I was intensely eager for a position in a Commonwealth public service graduate program. I applied everywhere I wanted to go, which included the Department of Defence, the Prime Minister's Department, and the Department of Foreign Affairs and Trade. Yet I was entirely unsuccessful and, inevitably, wounded in my numerous attempts.

Rather than despair, however, I created a long-range path toward my goal. What I needed was more experience. So I used my comparative advantage in sports by volunteering for an assignment running the organisation *Fiji Swimming* in Suva, Fiji. From here I built contacts with international development agencies and was recruited by the United Nations to work in PNG. During this time I also boosted my academic credentials (and picked up new professional skills) by completing a postgraduate certificate.

Experience 'on the ground' in two countries that are incredibly important to Australia naturally increased my chances of eventually winning a place in one of the most competitive graduate programs in the country. It's an instructive example of not losing hope but, most importantly, laying out a path toward achieving your targets.

Are you going to achieve all your goals? Perhaps not. But the fact that you possess targeted aspirations actually places you in a special league. 'The calamity isn't to have dreams unfulfilled,' the old saying goes, 'but to have no dreams to reach for.' And if you're intensely high-minded, there may be ideals you seek that are simply unachievable as an individual. These are, in the words of the writer David Brooks, 'tasks that can't be completed in a single lifetime.'

The most important thing to remember for young Australians is that, if you possess goals you truly aspire to, they won't fade with setback. Nor will you really lose your passion for them. Your goals will stay lit and, like the description of a dusty town in 2004, remain your 'ember in the ash heap.'

What's so great about Australia?

'There are far more tales of heroism and sacrifices in the penetration of the Australian outback,' notes the eminent historian Paul Johnson, 'than in the whole history of the American Far West.'

Such an accolade, from such a distinguished observer of history, is worth unwrapping for many younger Australians. Certainly, Australia is a unique nation. Few others in history have been as stable, prosperous or carry as special a heritage.

But we tend not to celebrate in a way that's expected of people rising to such heights from such humble beginnings. Indeed, ANZAC Day and Australia Day aside, moments of national pride are rarely expressed loudly. Our patriotism, thankfully, is subtle and not boisterous.

By examining the past we see the reasons for this. And we see what makes Australia a unique nation with traditions worth replicating, sustaining and taking advantage of.

America, the most powerful nation in history, was founded in 1620. But Australia was founded a century and a half later in 1788. A great deal happened in between that, arguably, set Australia up for a more successful start.

In 1687 Sir Isaac Newton, a candidate for the smartest person in history, produced *Principia Mathematica*, kick-starting the English Enlightenment and stoking an unmatched period of human innovation and enterprise. Under a spirit of progress and an expanding market economy the list of 'game-changing' inventions grew: telegraphy, photography, the rotary press, the telephone, the typewriter, the phonograph, the transatlantic cable, the electric light, movies, the locomotive, rockets, the steamboat, the x-ray, the revolver, and the stethoscope.

It was a unique and beneficial time to settle somewhere new. In 1788, the Sydney Harbour Bridge certainly didn't exist. There were no buildings, no streets and no airports. Not even a jetty or pontoon welcomed the First Fleet. Australia, as put by one historian, was a place where 'not a wheel had turned, no permanent structures existed and agriculture was unknown.'

But clearly the British, when arriving on Sydney's shores, had come to know a great deal about science, maths and health. Early Australians, with sheer hard work and self-agency, used this knowledge to farm, cultivate and offset the continent's jagged and stubborn contours. Through inventions like the stump jump plough, rust-resistant wheat, the Sunshine harvester and the Ridley stripper, Australia could grow and prosper.

This was a stark contrast to the Pilgrim Fathers settling the United States. A slim relative knowledge of science, agricultural techniques and medicine made their new enterprise miserable. The Pilgrim's first task, after a battering sea voyage without the aid of navigational instruments, was to settle the land. But no seed and primitive tactics meant a terrible start. At least a third of the Pilgrims died.

But in Australia, as the journalist Nick Cater observes, 'man's reason, observation and the power of science were present from the beginning.' While life was still extremely tough Australia's early years were largely more successful than America's. It was, in many ways, an enlightened start.

And it wasn't just on the land where Australia's achievements were built. Our institutions, crafted by ideas of liberty and freedom, emerged as unique. Slavery had become an affront to humanity. The law, unlike other times in human history, applied to everyone regardless of race, background or income.

There are a few tough and early examples of this. In 1788 – the year of arrival – the first convict was hanged for stealing. A year later six British naval marines were hanged for the same offence, sending a clear message that the rule of law applied 'across the board' regardless of social connection or occupation.

Within a few years the same message was received by anyone who might have thought that a victim's skin colour was relevant to the severity of the sentence. In 1797, for example, the first white man – John Kirby – was hanged for killing an Aborigine. A few decades later an appalled George Gipps, the Governor of New South Wales, ordered a retrial of the perpetrators of the 1838 Myall Creek Massacre. The offenders were sentenced and hanged.

While reigning in mob rule and applying the rule of law is now common, the standard practice of governance for centuries prior was one of arbitrary rule. Kings and Queens ruled by decree. The Magna Carta of 1215, however, established two radical but enduring ideas that would benefit Australia centuries later – due process and no taxation without representation.

An unbending commitment to these principles has been cited as a key reason for Australia's stability. 'There were no revolutionary uprisings,' writes Australian historian Peter Cochrane, 'no wars of independence, no fields of battle, no mud and blood, no great conspiracy or treason trials, no universe of practices and understandings swept away in a political whirlwind, and none of the attendant heroism called forth by such things.'

Without such turbulence Australia could pioneer world-beating reforms. 'The eight-hour day,' writes journalist Peter Hartcher, 'the secret ballot, the right of women to stand for parliament, the first workers' party to be elected to majority government – in these and the establishment of other rights for the common people, Australia was democracy's champion and history's pioneer.'

But Australia's extraordinary characteristics, I feel, don't ultimately lie in its governmental achievements but in its people. Sir Robert Menzies, Australia's longest serving Prime Minister, clearly understood the cascading and unique character of the Australian people. 'We have learned that true rising standards of living,' Menzies famously wrote, 'are the product of progressive enterprise, the acceptance of risks, the encouragement of adventure, the prospect of rewards. These are all individual matters. There is no Government department which can create these things.' Even at times of sheltered industry and political patronage such values of character, enterprise and economy have been lurking not far from the surface.

Indeed, there was clearly something special about the sheer drive, self-agency and industriousness of early Australians. Duty and sacrifice translated into a wartime commitment that, again, speaks to the core character of a unique nation. 'As a percentage of the population,' reflects one historian on the Second World War, 'almost twice as many Australians gave their lives as Americans, 0.57 per cent to 0.32 per cent. In the First World War it was more than ten times as many, 1.25 per cent to 0.11 per cent.' Yet rather than reflecting on such raw statistics with inflated pride we find humility, modest tones and capped self-celebration – a trait found across the Western hemisphere amid the expected jubilance of wartime victory.

In other ways we see this manifest in Australia through a lack of desire for pomp and ceremony. One of the first US Senates, for example, took a month to deliberate on the question of 'titles'. Australia, instead, opted for much more simplicity – a Crowned Republic. Today our political leaders, rather than celebrated with excessive flair, remain accessible custodians of the common will and everyday Australians.

In the realm of work and society, Australia's unwritten egalitarian code ensures that, rather than a master-client relationship, we've tended to possess an attitude of 'all hands on deck'. The reason for this, again, is found in our early years. 'The boss is the boss, certainly,' observes the Australian historian Geoffrey Dutton, 'but if he is any good he never asks a man to do what he cannot do himself.' Whether in the sheep yards, lamb-marking, cutting out cattle or bringing in a mob of sheep, Dutton writes of frontier life in the mid-1800s, 'at work everyone is in together.'

So, amid such a rich legacy, what's the message for young Australians today? I feel the biggest takeaway, among a very long list, is the ongoing reward for good and decent values. Regardless of the era, ideals of hard work and character will continue to propel Australians forward. These are things that don't have anything to do with race, skin colour, religion or income.

Nor are they related to excessive selfishness. Everyone, to echo Dutton's words, 'is in together.' Attachment, solidarity and the good bonds that exist between all Australians have shown that a sense of community is vital to achieving success. In fact, the nation's future entrepreneurs and opportunity creators will find that seeking ways to serve fellow patriots remains the best way to build prosperity and affluence.

All young Australians have a stake in ensuring that, just like earlier generations, they progress not just themselves but build a brighter future for their fellow Australians.

Conclusion

Thank you for reading *Winners Don't Cheat*. I hope the essays have been easy to follow and not too over-embellished with personal anecdote.

If you don't know better, as I wrote in the earlier pages, you can't do better. And that, of all the great messages within, is the prime takeaway I'd like you to have. For my start out of school 'knowing better' meant being exposed to a career of possibilities in places like Washington DC, our nation's parliament, reading widely, studying others, having the opportunity to travel and cultivating good people around me to keep the fuse lit.

I know that 'knowing better' isn't a sure fire way for success, and that all of the techniques here won't apply or work for you. But I hope *Winners Don't Cheat* can give you some place to apply these principles in your everyday life.

In closing, I finished with talking about Australian greatness because I feel that national success will continue to depend on the sum of individuals – how we counter adversity, build skill, innovate and contribute to our families, communities and friends. 'Leaners grow flabby,' said Australia's longest serving prime minister Robert Menzies, 'lifters grow muscles.' Menzies said these words in 1943 as part of his famous Forgotten People Lecture. But you'd be surprised how controversial this, and other advice espousing grit and resilience, has become. At a recent Lowy Institute future leadership discussion, for example, Menzies' quote was mocked by one of Australia's next generation leaders. *Winners Don't Cheat,*

I hope, gives some modern colour to how we can continue to be 'lifters' and not 'leaners'.

Good luck. Until next time.

Contact

Thank you for taking time to read *Winners Don't Cheat*. If you would like to read further or contact Sean please go to: www.seanjacobs.com.au.